SCHOLASTIC
CHOICES

Real stories
about drinking
and drugs

true
confessions

John DiConsiglio

Franklin Watts

AN IMPRINT OF SCHOLASTIC INC.
NEW YORK • TORONTO • LONDON • AUCKLAND • SYDNEY
MEXICO CITY • NEW DELHI • HONG KONG
DANBURY, CONNECTICUT

chapter one

6 Deadly Temptation

Drugs are dangerous and addicting. How do they get their hooks into teens? For Judy, one experience with heroin turned her life into a living nightmare.

chapter two

22 Drugs and the Brain

For many teens, drugs seem to offer relief, escape, and a good time. But what do drugs really do to your body? And what is addiction, anyway? Just ask Ricky about the horrible toll meth took on his life.

chapter three

38 Real Stories about Drugs and Alcohol

From cigarettes to alcohol, from heroin to steroids, from prescription meds to over-the-counter cough syrup, there are many drugs that can cause you harm. Learn the truth about these drugs.

NICOTINE:
Kevin's Story — 39

ALCOHOL:
Lacy's Story — 45

MARIJUANA:
Amanda's Story — 49

INHALANTS:
Megan's Story — 56

PRESCRIPTION DRUGS:
Nicole's Story — 62

STEROIDS:
Craig's Story — 67

COCAINE:
Blayze's Story — 73

ECSTASY:
Daniel's Story — 79

HEROIN:
Judy's Story — 84

METHAMPHETAMINE:
Ricky's Story — 86

chapter four

88 Clean and Sober

You can beat drugs and get your life back. Read how teens kicked the habit.

MORE INFORMATION

104 Glossary
106 Further Resources
108 Index
112 About the Author

deadly temptation

true
confessions

HOW MUCH DO YOU REALLY KNOW ABOUT DRUGS
AND THEIR EFFECT ON YOUR BODY, YOUR MIND,
AND YOUR LIFE? TAKE THIS TRUE-OR-FALSE QUIZ
TO TEST YOUR DRUG IQ.

True or False?

1 In some ways, cigarettes are as dangerous as drugs such as heroin— maybe even more so!

2 For teenagers, drugs are a bigger problem than alcohol.

3 Prescription drugs are never dangerous.

4 Inhalants can kill you, even if you only use them once or twice.

5 It's hard to quit drugs, alcohol, or cigarettes on your own. Treatment programs are more effective than going cold turkey.

Answers:

1. True. See page 42.
2. False. See page 47.
3. False. See page 65.
4. True. See page 58.
5. True. See page 91.

Photographs © 2008: Alamy Images: 16 (Siegfried Grassegger/imagebroker), 35 (PhotoAlto), 22 (Aliki Sapountzi/Aliki Image Library), 58 (sciencephotos); Corbis Images: 97 (H. Benser/zefa), 33 (Susanne Borges/A.B./zefa), 46 (David Burton/Beateworks), 25 (Jonathan Cavendish), 4 bottom, 80 (Emely/zefa), 27 (Robert Essel NYC), 51 (FURGOLLE/Image Point FR), 26 (Rick Gayle), 56, 57 (Ole Graf/zefa), 62 (Tom Grill), 8 (Edward Holub), 88 (Ted Horowitz), 90 (David Katzenstein), 4 top, 6 (Helen King), 98 (LaCoppola & Meier/zefa), 64 (Marianna Day Massey/ZUMA), 76, 84 (Mika/zefa), 42 (Jose Luis Pelaez, Inc.), 74 (Darius Ramazani/zefa), 30 (Roger Ressmeyer), 71 (Jim Richardson), 66 (Benjamin Rondel), 63 (Bill Ross), 100 (Alan Schein/zefa), 81 (Torleif Svensson), 86 (Turbo/zefa), 41 (Cathrine Wessel), 69 (John Wilkes Studio); Getty Images: 79 (Digital Vision), 77 (Holly Harris), 38 (Richard Koek), 45 (Seth Kushner), 10 (Debra McClinton), 52 (Jacopo Pandolfi), 94, 95 (Andy Reynolds), 49 (Eddie Soloway); JupiterImages/Eric Audras/PhotoAlto: 19; Monty Stilson: cover; PhotoEdit/Spencer Grant: 93; Photolibrary/Elea Dumas/Nonstock: 12; The Image Works/Bob Daemmrich: 69.

Cover design: Marie O'Neill
Book production: The Design Lab
CHOICES editor: Bob Hugel

Library of Congress Cataloging-in-Publication Data
DiConsiglio, John.
 True confessions : real stories about drinking and drugs / John DiConsiglio.
    p. cm.—(Scholastic choices)
 Includes bibliographical references and index.
 ISBN-13: 978-0-531-18848-4 (lib. bdg)   978-0-531-14773-3 (pbk)
 ISBN-10: 0-531-18848-5 (lib. bdg)   0-531-14773-8 (pbk)
 1. Teenagers—Drug use. 2. Teenagers—Alcohol use. 3. Drug abuse—Case studies. 4. Drug abuse—Prevention. I. Title.
 HV5824.Y68D533 2007
 613.8—dc22   2007012487

1 2 3 4 5 6 7 8 9 10 R 17 16 15 14 13 12 11 10 09 08

deadly temptation

"IT WASN'T EVEN 24 HOURS LATER, AND I WAS ALREADY CRAVING IT."

Heroin: Judy's Story

Judy was no stranger to drugs. By the time she was 15, she was smoking marijuana on a daily basis. She even tried ecstasy at a couple of parties. The Baltimore teen thought she was tough enough to handle anything that came her way. But this was like nothing she'd ever experienced. And suddenly, Judy was scared.

Judy was pressed into the mosh pit at a concert. The music was loud, and she couldn't hear what her boyfriend said as he passed her some marijuana. Or at least, she *thought* it was marijuana. But after a few puffs, Judy knew something was wrong.

"I felt this warm sensation flood over me, and then I went numb," says Judy, who is now 17. "The crowd was pushing me against the stage. I knew that I was getting squashed, but I couldn't feel a thing. That's what really freaked me out."

The next morning, Judy's boyfriend told her that he hadn't given her marijuana. It was heroin. Judy had always been afraid of heroin. So she was shocked to hear herself say, "I want to do it again."

Judy did not realize that she was already succumbing to drug **addiction**. Heroin "can lead to an intense addiction and dangerous behavior," says Dr. Catherine Sasek, of the National Institute on Drug Abuse (NIDA). "It has health risks that range from heart infections, liver disease, and breathing problems to lethal overdoses."

Like millions of teens, Judy was almost powerless to stop herself. "It wasn't even 24 hours later," she says, "and I was already craving it." What started as experimentation quickly escalated into an intense, uncontrollable need. "When you are on heroin," says Judy, "your whole life is getting high, getting sick, and then doing anything to get more drugs."

Hooked

Judy's parents split up when she was in middle school. Before the breakup, Judy always went to bed to the sounds of shouts and curses. To relieve the pain, she turned to marijuana. More and more, Judy smoked marijuana to escape reality. A bad grade on a test? A joint would make it go away. A fight with a friend? She'd forget all about it after a few puffs.

Judy always thought of herself as a middle-of-the-road kid. Her grades were fine. She tried soccer because everyone else did, but by seventh grade, she was bored with it. She wore jeans and T-shirts, not following any trends. In truth, she says, she never felt like she was much of anything. Until she started taking drugs. "At first, it was easier to do drugs than deal with my problems," she says. "But after a while, I was doing them because that's just what I did, who I was."

The day after she first smoked heroin, Judy snorted the drug with her boyfriend. "I never felt anything like it. It just made me all warm and numb and sleepy," she says. "But even that second time, I didn't feel the same rush as the first. And then I started needing more and more of it to get high."

Only a few hours after a heroin high wears off, people start craving more. Their bodies turn on them, and they suffer through nausea, vomiting, and diarrhea. "It's like the worst flu you've ever had—and then ten times worse than that," Judy says. "You think you are going to die. Even when you aren't sick, you're always a little pukey. Your skin feels uncomfortable on you, and you're always picking at it. The only thing that makes you feel better is more heroin."

Judy progressed from sampling heroin on the weekends to using it every day. She dropped out of school and spent all her time with her boyfriend and his heroin-addicted mother. On the rare occasions that she was home, Judy fought with her family. "My mother tried to get me to admit that I needed help, and I just beat her up," she says. "I can't believe I did that. But I was so wild. It wasn't me."

Just nine months after she first tried the drug, Judy was breaking into houses to steal anything she could trade for heroin. There was nothing else she wanted or cared about. "If things had kept going like they were," she says, "there's no doubt in my mind that I'd be dead today."

"There's no doubt in my mind that I'd be dead today."

By Any Other Name

It's hard to generalize about drugs and the teens who abuse them. Some drug addicts come from homes shattered by neglect. Others may be like the straight-A student sitting next to you at school. Some may take drugs as an escape from abuse. Others may take them simply because they're bored and want to try something new.

The teenage years are a time for experimentation. Whether it's new clothes, new hairstyles, or new friends, teens try to carve out new identities for themselves. In many ways, you're trying to figure out who you are—and who you're going to be. It's exciting and fun. But experimentation can sometimes go too far and become dangerous.

Sometimes it might seem as though drugs are everywhere—and that everyone is doing them. But the truth is that most teens do not use drugs. And the rate of teen drug use has steadily declined over the last decade.

Defining Drugs

So, what are drugs, anyway? Drugs are chemicals that affect your body. There are thousands of drugs that help people, such as antibiotics and vaccines, by treating or preventing diseases. But drugs can have harmful effects on people. Alcohol is a drug. Nicotine is also a drug. Though many drugs can be helpful when taken under a doctor's care, if you abuse drugs you risk harming yourself and becoming addicted.

Drug abuse is when you use substances that aren't prescribed to you by a doctor or take too much of ones that have been prescribed. Drug addiction is a dependency on drugs. When you're addicted, your body or mind—or both—craves the drug. In some cases, your body needs the drug just to keep you from feeling horribly sick. Ask an addict like Judy, and you'll learn that drug addiction is a frightening and dangerous disease.

a drug
LINEUP

Drugs aren't all the same. They have different effects on you and work on different parts of your brain. Here are the families of some well-known drugs.

Stimulants

Stimulants are drugs that act on the central nervous system and increase brain activity. Some give feelings of alertness, energy, and confidence. When these drugs' effects wear off, the user may experience intense hunger, anxiety, depression, as well as exhaustion.

- COCAINE AND CRACK
- AMPHETAMINES (such as methamphetamine)
- NICOTINE (in cigarettes, chewing tobacco, pipes, and cigars)

Depressants

Depressants are drugs that act on the central nervous system and slow down brain activity. They can impair coordination, balance, and judgment. Higher doses can lead to drowsiness, vomiting, coma, and even death.

- ALCOHOL
- TRANQUILIZERS (such as Valium, Ativan, Xanax, Rohypnol)
- GBH

Hallucinogens

Hallucinogens are drugs that change the way you experience the world through your five senses. Sometimes this involves seeing and hearing things that aren't there. These drugs can cause panic, paranoia, and an inability to make judgments.

- LSD
- PSILOCYBIN (such as hallucinogenic mushrooms)
- MDMA (such as ecstasy)

Opioids

Opioids are drugs that have effects similar to depressants and have a painkilling effect. Side effects can include slowed breathing, impaired judgment, nausea, vomiting, and constipation.

- **HEROIN**
- **PRESCRIPTION NARCOTICS (such as morphine, codeine, OxyContin, Percodan, Percocet)**

Cannabinoids

Cannabinoids are drugs derived from the cannabis plant that have stimulant, depressant, hallucinogenic, and intoxicating effects. Coordination and memory are impaired.

- **MARIJUANA**
- **HASHISH**

Inhalants

Inhalants are drugs administered by breathing in their vapors. These drugs usually reduce the amount of oxygen getting to the brain and can have a variety of effects.

- **VOLATILE SOLVENTS** (such as paint thinners, gasoline, glues, correction fluids)
- **AEROSOLS** (such as spray paints, deodorant sprays, hair sprays, cooking sprays)
- **GASES** (such as ether and nitrous oxide)
- **NITRITES** (such as amyl nitrite and butyl nitrite)

Anabolic steroids

Anabolic steroids are drugs that promote muscle growth and increase lean body mass. These drugs have medical uses and are often misused by people who want to bulk up and/or improve their athletic performance. Risks of abuse include mood swings and heart attacks.

- **NANDROLONE DECANOATE**
- **OXANDROLONE**
- **STANOZOLOL**

People of Influence

Drugs can be deadly. And drug addiction is a living nightmare. So why do so many young people fall into the grip of drug abuse? It's not an easy question to answer. In general, experts say that kids follow different influences, such as their friends and even the people they see on TV.

And the single most important influence on your life? You may not believe it, but it's your parents. In about 80 percent of cases, a child's first exposure to alcohol and drug use is in the home. Parents may have a liquor cabinet, a steady supply of beer in the refrigerator, a pack of cigarettes in the glove compartment, or other drugs in the home.

According to a 2001 study by the National Institutes of Health (NIH), teens' relationships with their parents are also a major factor in whether they will use drugs. "Teens who perceived that their parents like them, respect them, take them seriously, listen to them and give reasons for rules and decisions that involve them were less likely to smoke and drink," the report says.

Drug addiction is a dependency on drugs

After your parents, your friends are as influential as anyone. For most teenagers, friends become as close—if not closer—than family. You tell your friends all your secrets and dreams. And if your friends are doing drugs, you probably feel pressure to do them, too.

In fact, the 2001 NIH study found that girls and boys who associated with friends who smoke and drink were more likely to do the same. The study also showed that girls were more susceptible than boys to drinking and using drugs because of peer pressure.

"You can't understate the role that friends play in kids' lives," says Kimberley O'Brien, a therapist and expert on teen drug addiction from Vancouver, Canada. "It's very hard for a young person to go against the things their crowd does. They don't want to feel like outcasts."

Pressure Cooker

Another reason kids say they take drugs is to relieve the pressures they feel in their lives—both inside their bodies and outside.

Many young people "self-medicate" with drugs; they take drugs to deal with intense feelings such as stress, low self-worth, depression, anxiety, and nervousness. Alcohol and drugs are mood-altering substances. But drugs only mask these problems; they don't solve them. "You are trying to cure one problem, and, in the process, creating another," O'Brien says. "Drugs simply hide feelings and problems. When they wear off, the problem is still there— or it's worse. And now you have additional problems."

Some kids use drugs when the external pressures of everyday life seem to become overwhelming. They hope the drugs will relieve the stress of school, fights with their friends, family problems, or the end of a relationship. They may even think drugs and alcohol give them courage to be more social and outgoing.

TEENS at Risk

It's true that there are some serious risk factors for teens, such as a family history of substance abuse, depression, and low self-esteem. But those aren't the only reasons kids take drugs, says Jean Kopner, a child psychologist from Dallas, Texas. "Some kids stumble into drugs," she says. "They aren't really taking them for an escape. It's much less devious than that. They start taking them for what seem like petty reasons. And many times, they become a part of their lives."

Indeed, Kopner says her teen patients often list these reasons for taking drugs:

- They're curious about the effects.

- The drugs are readily available; a friend had them or they were used casually at a party.

- They have already started drinking but can't get— or can't afford—alcohol.

- They tried it once and enjoyed the short-term effects.

- "Club drugs"—like ecstasy—are part of their music scene.

- They want to "break the rules." Using drugs or alcohol makes them feel rebellious and independent. It may also make them feel grown up.

- They are bored. They live somewhere that doesn't offer many other things to do for fun.

drugs
and the
brain

drugs and the brain

"I THOUGHT I COULD HANDLE IT."

Meth Addict's Diary: Ricky's Story

I was just a normal 17-year-old kid—a good student who never got into any trouble. I volunteered at a nursing home, my mother and I were practically best friends, and I was my little sister's hero. But after less than year of smoking crystal meth, I'm a different person. I look like a ghost, with sunken cheeks and little black holes for eyes. I haven't been to school in weeks. My sisters hate me. My mother cries for me every night. I'm addicted to methamphetamine.

The summer before my senior year, I made the worst mistake of my life. Some friends were hanging out at an older guy's house. I knew he smoked meth. He even asked me if I wanted to try it. I always told him no. I don't know what made me finally say yes. I thought about those drug lectures, how they kept telling us that meth would drive you crazy. But this guy didn't look so bad.

From my first hit of crystal meth, I suddenly knew everything was different. That initial flash of the drug in my head nearly knocked me down. It gave me this incredible energy, like an adrenaline rush or a roller coaster ride. It messes with your mind. I remember thinking, "This is the best feeling of my life."

I stayed up for two days high on meth. I couldn't sit still. I cleaned the house. I played video games until my fingers were sore. I did books of crossword puzzles. I finally crashed and slept

"That initial flash of the drug in my head nearly knocked me down."

"For the next nine months, crystal meth ruled my life."

through a whole day. When I woke up, my first thought was, "Wow, I want to do that again."

For the next nine months, crystal meth ruled my life. All I wanted to do was binge and crash. I smoked it every chance I could. I tried to hide it from people. But meth makes you stop eating. By the time school started, I was rail thin with sunken eyes and slumped shoulders.

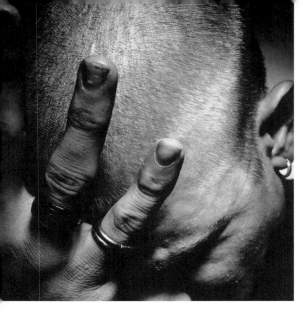

I thought I could handle it. When you are high on meth, you think you can do anything. I was awake for five or six days at a time, so tweaked out that I'd do my homework again and again. When I finally crashed, I'd sleep like a corpse for days. One day, I stumbled out of bed, grating my teeth and scratching at my arms. My mom asked me point-blank, "Have you tried crystal meth?" I came clean. "Mom," I said, "I've been high on it for months."

My family was shattered. My mother begged me to get help. My little sister cried and screamed at me. But I didn't care. Nothing was more important to me than crystal meth. I forged checks to get money for the drug. I broke into cars and shoplifted. I'd take anything—spare change, laptops, clothes. Anything I could trade for more meth.

One night, my mother hid my car keys. I threw her to the ground in a rage. She called the police, and I spent my first night in jail. Then there was the time I got into a fight with my stepfather. I was arrested again and sent to juvenile detention for four days. When I was finally released, I had to wear an electronic monitor.

I promised everyone I would clean up my act. And I meant it. I even got a job. But two weeks later, I cashed my first paycheck. Without thinking twice, I bought meth and stayed up all night smoking it. My mom woke up the next morning and found me still in my clothes, looking like a truck hit me. She made me call my probation officer. Fifteen minutes later, a police car came for me. Then, a court ordered me into rehab.

DRUG = compulsively seeking out a drug
addiction

Addicted!

For Ricky, meth became an all-consuming passion. He craved more and more—even as the drug destroyed his family, his body, and his life. Drug addiction causes a person to compulsively seek out a drug—whether it's alcohol, nicotine, or heroin. The addict craves it. Everything else—family, friends, school—becomes secondary to the drug. To many people, drug addicts seem sad and pathetic. Others are disgusted by them and their lack of self-control. Why, people wonder, can't they just stop?

Scientists now realize that drug addiction is a disease, and that some people may be more at risk for this disease than others. No one factor can predict why some kids become drug addicts and some don't. But your genes may account for 40 percent to 60 percent of your vulnerability to addiction. There is also evidence that people with mental illness have a much greater risk of drug abuse and addiction.

"Drug addiction isn't just a matter of willpower," says Dr. Nora D. Volkow, director of NIDA. "It is a brain disease." And quitting drugs isn't easy. Drugs make long-lasting chemical changes in your brain. Once you start taking an addictive drug, your brain begins to work differently. Without a dose of the drug, the levels of some natural chemicals in an addict's brain are lower than they should be. The person feels flat, lifeless, and depressed. Getting your brain back on track isn't easy.

"Drug addiction isn't just a matter of willpower."

To understand exactly how drugs affect your mind, we first have to take a look inside your head and understand how your brain works.

Brain Scan: What's Really Going On Inside Your Head?

The brain is the command center of your body. It controls every move you make. That's amazing, considering it only weighs 3 pounds (1.4 kilograms)—about the same as a chihuahua.

The brain's job is to process information. Everything you know and everything you do goes through the brain. Your brain conveys messages to your body through cells called

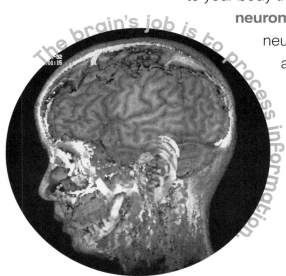

neurons. There are billions of neurons in the human brain, all flashing messages to each other.

A message travels through a neuron as an electrical impulse. This impulse triggers the

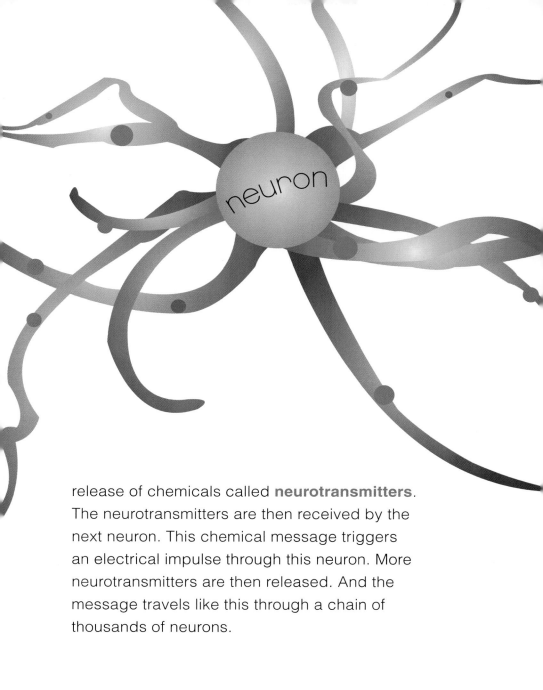

neuron

release of chemicals called **neurotransmitters**.
The neurotransmitters are then received by the
next neuron. This chemical message triggers
an electrical impulse through this neuron. More
neurotransmitters are then released. And the
message travels like this through a chain of
thousands of neurons.

LIMBIC SYSTEM = **reward center**

The Limbic System

At the top of your brain is an area called the **cerebral cortex**. It's the thinking center. That's where you store and process things like language, math, and your ability to make a plan and think ahead. Buried deep within the cerebral cortex is the **limbic system**. It plays an important role: it tells us what we like. In a sense, the limbic system is responsible for our survival. It remembers and creates an appetite for the things that you like and that keep you alive, such as food and friendship.

The limbic system is often called the brain's reward system. It responds when good things happen, like when your team wins a baseball game or you eat a great meal or someone compliments you on your new haircut.

Feelings of pleasure and satisfaction cause the limbic system to release a neurotransmitter called

dopamine. Because natural pleasures in life
are necessary for survival, the limbic system drives
you to seek out the things that have made you feel
good. Any experience or activity that results in the
release of dopamine becomes something that you
will want to do again.

How Drugs Trick Your Brain

Drugs affect the natural workings of your brain. Remember, dopamine is the neurotransmitter that the limbic system releases when something good happens. Many drugs increase the amount of dopamine in your brain. If you take these drugs, your brain is tricked into thinking that you are doing something good.

Your brain also remembers feelings of pleasure, including those produced by drugs. It strives to repeat those feelings. In other words, it starts to crave the good feelings that the drug gave it. And the only way to repeat those feelings is to take more drugs.

After enough doses, the limbic system of an addicted teen craves the drug just as it craves food, water, or friends. Without a dose of the drug, dopamine levels in the addict's brain are low. The addict becomes sluggish and depressed.

But by now, the addict has developed a **tolerance** to the drug. That means they need more and more of the drug just to get the same effect the addict once got on the first high. Addicted teens have changed the way their brains work. And those changes have made them lose the ability to control their drug use.

Without a dose of the drug, dopamine levels in the addict's brain are LOW. **The addict becomes** SLUGGISH **and** DEPRESSED.

The Truth about
DRUG ADDICTION: FAQs

Addiction versus abuse

QUESTION: Is there a difference between abuse and addiction? Are all substance abusers addicts?

ANSWER: There is a difference—but abuse often leads to addiction. Abuse is when a person takes a drug for non-medical reasons. Addiction means a person has no control over whether he or she uses a drug.

Physical versus psychological

QUESTION: What's the difference between a physical and a psychological addiction?

ANSWER: Physical addiction is when a person's body actually becomes dependent on a particular substance. When a person who is physically addicted stops using the drug, withdrawal symptoms—such as diarrhea, shaking, high fever, and nausea—are common. People who are psychologically addicted feel overcome by the psychological or emotional desire to have a drug. They feel as if they can't cope without it and may lie or steal to get it.

First time?

QUESTION: Can teens become addicted the first time they try a drug?

ANSWER: No one knows how many doses of a drug cause a person to become addicted. Your brain changes the very first time you use a drug. Genetic makeup probably plays a role in determining how fast a person becomes addicted. And psychologically, you can probably yearn for a drug after only one use.

Teens versus adults

QUESTION: Are teens more likely to become addicts than adults?

ANSWER: There is some evidence that teenagers are more at risk for drug problems than adults. Addiction usually begins in adolescence, or even childhood, when the brain is still developing. The part of your brain that governs judgment and decision making doesn't fully develop until your 20s. The limbic system develops earlier. That "reward" system influences a young person's decisions more than it does an adult's—putting you at greater risk of drug addiction.

real stories about drugs and alcohol

real stories about drugs and alcohol

"I WANT TO QUIT. I'M TRYING TO QUIT. BUT IT'S NOT THAT EASY."

Nicotine: Kevin's Story

If you're looking for Kevin and his high school baseball team during fourth-period lunch—and sometimes through the start of fifth-period history—don't bother searching the cafeteria or the practice diamond. On most afternoons, you'll find a handful of the top players from this Virginia high school team huddled with twenty other students in a friend's nearby basement rec room. They eat pizza. They play video games. And always—always—they smoke cigarettes.

"Kids hanging out. Whether it's a party or lunch, there are going to be smokes," says Kevin, an 18-year-old senior and a regular attendee at the basement hangout. Kevin is a star member of the school's golf team. He was also an ace pitcher until he tore a ligament in his knee.

And until recently, he smoked two packs of cigarettes a day.

"People always ask me, How can you run so fast, throw so far, play golf so well, and be such a heavy smoker?" says Kevin, who has cut his daily habit down to ten cigarettes. "I want to quit. I'm trying to quit. But it's not that easy."

"Kevin's story is not unusual," says Dr. Bill Corrigall, director of NIDA's Nicotine and Tobacco Addiction Program. "Many teens and even preteens begin to experiment with smoking but soon find they are smoking regularly—they're addicted."

More than ever, teens find that the best way to stop smoking is to never start at all. Teen smoking rates have fallen steadily since 1996, according to a NIDA-funded study.

That's the good news. The bad news, experts say, is that teen smoking numbers are still too high.

Each day, more than 3,000 children and adolescents become cigarette smokers, according to the Centers for Disease Control and Prevention. That's more than a million teens a year. Roughly one-third of them will die from a smoking-related illness.

THE **TRUTH** ABOUT
nicotine:
FAQs

QUESTION Are cigarettes as dangerous as other drugs like heroin or cocaine?

ANSWER In some ways, cigarettes are as dangerous as other drugs. Cigarette smoke contains more than 4,000 chemicals, including toxins like ammonia. But the chief culprit in cigarettes is nicotine, a powerfully addictive drug. Like cocaine and heroin, nicotine stimulates the release of too much dopamine, which changes the way your brain functions and leads to addiction.

QUESTION Is smoking as dangerous for teens as it is for adults?

ANSWER Research suggests that nicotine is even more harmful to the developing heart, lungs, and brains of teens. That's bad news because about nine out of ten tobacco users start before they're 18 years old.

QUESTION How many teens smoke?

ANSWER In 2005, about 13 percent of teens had smoked in the last 30 days, as opposed to about 42 percent in 1998, according to the surgeon general. Only 8 percent were "frequent" smokers. Unfortunately, 3,000 young people start smoking every day.

QUESTION If I smoke, how likely is it to seriously affect my health?

ANSWER More than a million teens a year start smoking—and about a third of them will die from a tobacco-related illness such as cancer, emphysema, or heart disease. Cigarette smoking accounts for about a third of all cancer deaths and 90 percent of all lung cancer deaths. One survey showed that a single cigarette takes about 5–20 minutes off your life.

QUESTION Are other forms of nicotine as addictive or harmful as cigarettes?

ANSWER Several forms of nicotine are just as deadly as cigarettes. They include chewing tobacco, cigars, and bidis (flavored, unfiltered cigarettes).

Kevin's Story Continued

Kevin started smoking the way most kids do. He'd seen his parents smoke. His older brother lit up. And by middle school, his friends always seemed to be sneaking away for a cigarette.

"I didn't think I was the kind of kid who would be so influenced by peer pressure," he says. "But it took me over before I realized it." Kevin didn't set out to be a chain smoker. The first time he smoked a cigarette, he didn't even like it. It burned his throat and made him feel sick. But it didn't take long for cigarettes to become a daily habit. And Kevin says he feels the effects. "I used to be able to run a mile in under six minutes. Now I'm lucky to make it in eight. And I'm wheezing all the way."

"Teens have a choice: They can become victims, or they can stop before they go too far," says Dr. Eric Moolchan, director of NIDA's Teen Tobacco Addiction Treatment Research Clinic. "Better yet, they never have to start at all."

> TEENS HAVE A **CHOICE**:
> They can become victims, or they can stop before they go too far.

Alcohol: Lacy's Story

Eighth-grader Lacy never drank at all. Well, she took some sips from her parents' liquor cabinet when she was in sixth grade. But she didn't even like the taste of alcohol. But as Lacy became more and more involved with Peter, a high school junior, her personality changed. She started listening to the kind of music he liked. And she started drinking with him at parties. First, it was just a little beer on the weekends. Lacy soon realized that she liked drinking. She liked the dizzy feeling that alcohol gave her.

Every Saturday night seemed to end the same way. Lacy would pass out at a friend's party. Someone would have to get her home. The next day, she'd wake up with a pounding headache and little memory of what had happened the night before. Still, she never thought she had an alcohol problem. "I was a good kid," she says. "I was like, 'so I drink on the weekends. What's the big deal?'"

"I was a good kid. I was like, 'so I drink on the weekends. What's the big deal?'"

THE **TRUTH** ABOUT
alcohol:
FAQs

QUESTION Is alcohol really considered a drug?

ANSWER Yes. Whether it's beer, wine, or liquor, alcohol acts on nerve cells in the brain just like any other drug. Also like other drugs, alcohol can be addictive. One study found that about 40 percent of people who started drinking at age 13 or younger developed alcohol dependency later in life.

QUESTION Don't most teenagers drink?

ANSWER Fewer than half of all teens drank alcohol in 2003. The number of teens abusing alcohol continues to drop, as it has nearly every year since 1999. About 28 percent of kids said they had been binge drinking (at least five drinks in a row) in the last two weeks. That's down more than 5 percent over a 10-year period.

QUESTION Is alcohol really a big problem compared with other drugs?

ANSWER Alcohol is the number-one drug problem of today's teens. It kills more young people than cocaine, heroin, and every other illegal drug combined. Teens who have been drinking are more likely to get into cars with other drunk teens. Car accidents are the leading cause of death for teenagers. And while teen drinking has dropped, many kids still aren't getting the message. Nearly half of all Americans over the age of 12 consume alcohol. There are 10–15 million alcoholics in the United States—and as many as 4.5 million of them are teens.

QUESTION As long as I don't get into a car, what's the worst thing that can happen to me if I drink a lot?

ANSWER Too much drinking can lead to alcohol poisoning. That's when alcohol has so dulled your nerves that your breathing can stop. It also shuts off your gag reflex, so if you vomit, you could choke to death. Teens who drink are more likely to make bad decisions.

QUESTION What are the long-term physical effects of alcohol abuse?

ANSWER Alcohol abuse over time can cause many health problems: heart problems; breathing dangers; increased risk of mouth and throat cancer; damage to the gastrointestinal system, the pancreas, and the kidneys; and severe liver disease, which kills as many as 25,000 Americans each year.

Lacy's Story Continued

Lacy still considered herself a casual drinker until Peter broke up with her. That's when she started drinking more heavily. She didn't drink just at weekend parties. She drank after school with friends. Sometimes she downed a quick beer on her way to school in the morning.

Lacy didn't stop drinking. "I wasn't sure if I could at that point," she says. Her problem finally came to a head at a friend's party. Someone brought a bottle of whiskey, stolen from a parent's liquor cabinet. Most of the kids had a few sips. But Lacy drank almost the entire bottle—along with a few beers. "It was like I couldn't stop," she says. She remembers making out with some boys she barely knew. But the rest of the night is a blur.

"I just blacked out."

Her friends dumped her in a backyard. But a neighbor saw her lying face down in the grass and called

Lacy was dying of alcohol poisoning. They pumped her stomach to save her life.

the police. They hurried her to a hospital. Lacy was dying of alcohol poisoning. Doctors pumped her stomach to save her life. "I could have died," she says. Lucy had also damaged her relationship with her parents. "I don't know if they'll ever trust me again," she says.

Marijuana: Amanda's Story

I giggled when I drove into the first garbage can. "Ten points," I said. Then I hit another—harder. Everyone in the car laughed. I was driving—well, swerving, really—in my girlfriend's car. I aimed at a garbage can and hit the gas. Then I slammed on the brakes and drove slow. Very slow. Maybe ten miles an hour. Behind me, cars honked and flashed their lights. My friends and I just laughed louder as I veered all over the road. It was hard to see. The car was filled with smoke. And besides, I'd forgotten to turn on the headlights.

"Behind me, cars honked and flashed their lights. My friends and I just laughed louder as I veered all over the road. It was hard to see. The car was filled with smoke."

I'm 17 now. And I haven't used pot—or any other drug—in almost a year. But since I first tried marijuana at 14, I smoked it on a daily basis. There's a lot of things about smoking pot that I really regret. I failed most of my classes and ruined my reputation as a good student—and a good kid. My parents lost their trust in me. I lost interest in everything I used to love, like going to art museums or making jewelry.

And right at the top of my list of regrets is getting high and getting behind the wheel of a car. Once I hit a street sign and I lost my front tooth. I ended up in the emergency room with a cap in my mouth and back pain that still won't go away. But it could have been much worse. I could have killed myself—or someone else.

"It could have been much worse. I could have killed myself—or someone else."

THE **TRUTH** ABOUT
marijuana:
FAQs

QUESTION How can something natural, like marijuana, still be bad for you?

ANSWER There are a lot of chemicals in marijuana—about 400 of them, some of which can cause lung cancer. The THC in marijuana increases dopamine levels in your brain, just like other drugs.

QUESTION I know my parents smoked marijuana in college. How bad can it really be?

ANSWER The marijuana you buy today is a lot stronger and a lot more dangerous. The THC content of marijuana averaged less than 1 percent in 1974. By 1994, it was 4 percent. Today, it's anywhere from 7.5 percent to 24 percent. The more THC in marijuana, the greater the risk of damage to your brain and body.

QUESTION Can smoking marijuana affect my schoolwork?

ANSWER Marijuana affects your memory, which makes it harder to learn and do your schoolwork. Users experience short-term memory loss because the drug attaches itself to the hippocampus, the part of the brain involved in learning and memory.

QUESTION Is marijuana addictive?

ANSWER In 2002, more than 280,000 people went into drug treatment programs with what they called a marijuana addiction. Teens who use marijuana can become psychologically dependent. There's some debate over whether your body can develop a physical addiction to marijuana.

QUESTION How many kids smoke marijuana?

ANSWER Most teenagers do not use marijuana. In a recent poll, about one in six tenth graders said they were current users. Fewer than one in four high school seniors reported being a current user. Also, since 1996, marijuana use has declined slowly. Teens were as much as a third less likely to start smoking marijuana as they were a decade before.

QUESTION What are the harmful effects of marijuana?

ANSWER Marijuana elevates your heart rate and blood pressure. The drug can make you paranoid or cause you to hallucinate. It can impair coordination, concentration, and perception, which can lead to risky decisions such as unsafe sex. Marijuana diminishes your short-term memory.

Other harmful effects of marijuana use are damaged lungs and airways, increased susceptibility to respiratory diseases, and a damaged immune system. Marijuana can also cause changes in hormones that can delay the onset of puberty in men and may disrupt menstrual cycles in women.

QUESTION Is driving after smoking marijuana as dangerous as drinking and driving?

ANSWER Driving after smoking marijuana is every bit as dangerous as drunk driving. Marijuana makes drivers disoriented. They can miss turning cars or vehicles merging onto the highway. Marijuana hurts your peripheral vision and depth perception. Still, one in six high school seniors admits to driving after smoking marijuana. What's more, teens often don't understand the danger of smoking and driving. Forty-one percent of teens say they aren't concerned about getting in a car with a drugged driver.

Amanda's Story Continued

After I went to the ER, my parents got me into rehab. They sent me to a drug-treatment facility for teens in Michigan. I'm back in school and getting good grades. My teachers are amazed. My relationship with my parents is good again. I'm even looking forward to going to college next fall. I want to be a kindergarten teacher, like my mom.

But I still think about those nights when the smoke filled my girlfriend's car. I'd sit behind the wheel with a joint, pretending I was inside my own personal video game. Ten points for crashing into a garbage can. Twenty for knocking down a mailbox. We'd giggle as the wheels slipped on the ice. It was one big party on wheels. If you saw us out on the road those nights, well, I hope you kept your distance. It might have saved your life.

"I'm even looking forward to going to college next fall. I want to be a kindergarten teacher, like my mom."

Inhalants: Megan's Story

Until she was 12, Megan had a simple life in her small South Dakota town. She grew up with one mall and one movie theater. She describes herself as a "regular, happy kid" who hung out with friends and watched TV.

Then things got complicated. Megan was sexually abused by a trusted friend. "I thought about it a lot, and I didn't know what to do. I wanted it to go away," she says. Too afraid to tell her parents and unsure of how to cope with her feelings, she tried to escape her pain. A friend showed her how to get high using inhalants.

Megan and a group of friends began "huffing" together often. Her friends quit when they learned that huffing can kill you. But Megan kept huffing. Her whole sense of self-worth was out of whack after the sexual abuse. "I figured why not hurt myself, if he hurt me," she said.

"I thought about it a lot, and I didn't know what to do. I wanted it to go away."

THE **TRUTH** ABOUT
inhalants:
FAQs

QUESTION Can one or two uses of inhalants hurt you?

ANSWER You can die the very first time you try inhalants. It's common enough that there's even a name for this phenomenon: Sudden Sniffing Death. When you breathe in the fumes, you fill up the cells in your lungs with poisonous chemicals, leaving no room for the oxygen you need to breathe. Lack of oxygen— asphyxiation—can lead to respiratory failure and death. Approximately 100 teens die each year from inhalant abuse.

QUESTION How many kids abuse inhalants?

ANSWER About 2 million kids between the ages of 12 and 17 have abused inhalants at least once in their life. And an amazing 6 percent of young children have tried huffing by the time they reach fourth grade. The percentage of eighth graders who said they'd tried inhalants jumped from 15.8 percent in 2003 to 17.3 percent in 2004.

Are inhalants as dangerous as other drugs?

ANSWER Inhalants can have deadly and irreversible effects. Toluene, the active ingredient in many inhalants, strips the protective sheath off nerve cells in the brain. That literally shrinks the brain, causing muscle spasms and tremors. You can even have permanent difficulty with basic actions like walking, bending, and talking. Other inhalants, such as benzene (found in gasoline) can cause bone marrow damage.

QUESTION **How can nitrous oxide be dangerous if dentists use it?**

ANSWER When abused, nitrous oxide can be as dangerous as any other inhalant. Dentists never give pure nitrous oxide to patients. They always mix it with oxygen. When you breathe in pure nitrous oxide, it binds with the oxygen in your blood and your body's tissues can't get the oxygen they need. It can damage your peripheral nerves, causing numbness, tingling, and even paralysis. It also causes dangerous blackouts.

ANSWER All inhalants are different. Here's a list of inhalant types, where they come from, and their harmful effects:

INHALANT: Toluene
SOURCES: Spray paint, glue, fingernail polish
EFFECTS: Hearing loss, damage to central nervous system, liver and kidney damage

INHALANT: Trichloroethylene
SOURCES: Cleaning fluid, correction fluid
EFFECTS: Hearing loss, liver and kidney damage, vision loss

INHALANT: Hexane
SOURCES: Glue, gasoline
EFFECTS: Nerve damage resulting in chronic limb spasms, blackouts

INHALANT: Nitrous Oxide
SOURCES: Whipped cream dispensers, gas cylinders
EFFECTS: Nerve damage resulting in chronic limb spasms, blackouts

INHALANT: Benzene
SOURCES: Gasoline
EFFECTS: Bone marrow damage, immune system damage

Megan's Story Continued

It wasn't just Megan's brain cells that were in danger when she started huffing. She ignored her schoolwork. Her best friend dumped her because of the drug use. And she lashed out at her mom. "I always hit my mom when I was using," says Megan. "I feel really bad because I should have never hit my mom. That's something that nobody should ever do."

Megan hit rock bottom one night. High on inhalants and other drugs, she rode on top of a friend's car, fell off, and got a concussion. Then rock bottom got even lower. The next night, she fought with her brother. He said she was an embarrassment to the family. That struck a chord with Megan. "I knew it was true, but I didn't want to hear it," she says.

Megan finally got into a treatment facility. Today, she's 16, and she's been inhalant-free for almost two years. But things are not as simple as they once were. She still suffers from some of the effects of her inhalant abuse. "I can't really remember a lot of things," she says. "When I'm talking, I'll forget what I just said two seconds before. It frustrates me a lot." She says she now appreciates every day because she knows that she is one of the lucky ones who survived.

Megan's story is adapted from "Pain Meets Poison," by Cate Baily, *Junior Scholastic*, March 14, 2003.

Prescription Drugs: Nicole's Story

Nicole says she became addicted to Xanax at age 16, the minute a boyfriend gave her one pill. "It made me forget everything. It made me feel . . . nothing," she says. After weeks of almost constant use of Xanax, her grades were plummeting and her close relationship with her mom was in tatters. "All I wanted to do," she says, "was take those 'bars.'"

"All I wanted to do was take those 'bars.'"

One day, Nicole was called to the principal's office. Immediately, she knew she was in trouble. And this wasn't talking-in-class trouble. This was serious trouble. Two police officers were sent to escort her from fifth period to the school office. And Nicole knew why.

She was carrying fifty-nine pills, little white rectangles that kids at her Texas high school called "xanbars", or "bars" for short. The xanbars were Xanax, a depressant prescribed to treat anxiety and stress. Nicole had planned to take some of the pills and sell the rest to her classmates.

In a panic, Nicole shoved the pills down her jeans. But the cops stopped her with ten pills still in her hand. She was arrested for illegally possessing prescription medication.

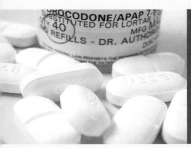

THE **TRUTH** ABOUT
prescription drugs:
FAQs

QUESTION Is prescription drug abuse really a big problem?

ANSWER The abuse of pharmaceutical drugs has become the fastest-growing drug problem in the United States. A 2005 Columbia University study found that more than 15 million Americans—or 6 percent of people in the country—admit to abusing prescription drugs. That's more than all other forms of drug abuse combined.

QUESTION How many teens abuse prescription drugs?

ANSWER Prescription drug abuse has skyrocketed among Americans, especially teens. After marijuana use, abuse of prescription drugs is the most common form of drug use reported by teenagers. About 14 percent of high school seniors have used prescription drugs for nonmedical reasons, notes a 2004 University of Michigan survey.

QUESTION Aren't drugs that are prescribed by a doctor safe?

ANSWER Prescription drugs have helped millions of people with problems from depression to cancer, but if not taken responsibly, they can land you in the emergency room—or the morgue. Prescribed medicines are custom fit to each patient's medical history, weight, allergies, etc., so it's unsafe—not to mention illegal—to take anyone else's prescriptions. Also, many prescription drugs are just as addictive as illegal drugs.

QUESTION Is it dangerous to combine prescription medications or to take them with alcohol?

ANSWER Combining drugs is always a very dangerous risk. Alcohol is no exception, and neither are prescription drugs. Every drug is different— some slow down your heart rate and others speed it up. Mixing them can be lethal.

QUESTION Aren't over-the-counter medicines (which don't require prescriptions) like cough and cold medicines safe—even if you take very high doses?

ANSWER Taken in high doses, over-the-counter medicines can be lethal. Many cold medicines contain a chemical called dextromethorphan (DXM). It depresses the central nervous system, somewhat like an opiate. When taken in large doses, it causes hallucinations, and it can also cause heart attacks or respiratory problems.

Nicole's Story Continued

Nicole was arrested and kicked out of school for abusing prescription drugs. She spent some time in jail on drug charges. Now she's in rehab.

Nicole is working hard to get back to school. Her mom is sticking by her, but her brothers won't talk to her. And she doesn't dare tell her father about her drug use. "He would never forgive me," she says.

Nicole had wanted to be a police officer. But with a felony drug charge on her record, she'll have to set her sights on another dream. "It was just two stupid years that I took those pills, and they ruined the rest of my life," she says. "If I could go back again, I'd change everything. I never would have gotten involved with those pills."

"If I could go back again, I'd change everything. I never would have gotten involved with those pills."

Steroids: Craig's Story

Every time Craig passed a mirror, he flexed his muscles. He wanted to look "insanely big—like an action figure."

"When I walked into a room, I wanted heads to turn," he says. People did notice Craig's 225-pound, five-foot-nine frame. But what they didn't see was the physical damage and psychological turmoil going on inside. The story behind the bulk was five years of steroid abuse.

"WHEN I WALKED INTO A ROOM, I WANTED HEADS TO TURN."

It all started when Craig was 18. Before a trip to Disney World, he was feeling overweight. He wanted to look good with his shirt off, so he resolved to get fit. Running on a treadmill, he slimmed down fast, losing 20 pounds in a month.

But that wasn't enough. "I wanted people to say, 'That guy's huge,'" Craig said. He lifted weights and experimented with steroidal supplements, also called dietary supplements. These drugs promise to build muscles. Despite potential risks and questionable effectiveness, they can be bought over the counter at many stores.

Still, Craig didn't feel that he was building muscle fast enough. So he turned to anabolic steroids, drugs derived from the male sex hormone testosterone.

To use steroids as Craig did is illegal. But like 4 percent of high school seniors and an estimated hundreds of thousands of adults, he took steroids anyway. Craig thought he knew exactly what he was getting into, but he wasn't ready for the grim reality of what steroids could do to his body and his mind.

THE **TRUTH** ABOUT
steroids:
FAQs

QUESTION Doctors prescribe steroids. Aren't they legal?

ANSWER Nonmedical use of steroids is illegal. There are legitimate medical uses for steroids—they can be prescribed to treat asthma, chronic lung disease, skin conditions, and severe allergic reactions. But doctors never prescribe anabolic steroids to young, healthy people.

QUESTION Will steroids improve my appearance?

ANSWER You may bulk up, but steroids will cause freakish appearance changes. In boys, steroids can cause enlarged breasts, shrunken testicles, baldness, and sterility. In girls, steroids can cause irreversible deepening of the voice, shrinking breasts, menstrual irregularities, baldness, and hair growth on other parts of the body including the face. Steroid users of both genders often get outbreaks of pimples on their backs. In addition, steroids can stunt users' growth. Teens who use steroids may never reach their full adult height.

QUESTION Can steroids damage my health?

ANSWER Steroids can wreak havoc with your body. They can cause liver damage or cancer. Steroid abusers can develop blood-filled sacs in the liver that can rupture and cause internal bleeding. Abusing steroids can cause heart attacks and strokes, even in young athletes. Steroids can also weaken the immune system. And by injecting steroids with needles, teens put themselves at risk of contracting HIV and **hepatitis**.

QUESTION Is "roid rage" real?

ANSWER Roid rage is a term for the uncontrolled aggression and violent behavior brought on by steroids. The drugs affect the limbic system, the part of the brain that's involved in emotions and moods. Steroids can make users irritable, depressed, manic, and delusional.

QUESTION Can steroids be addicting?

ANSWER Steroid use can lead to addiction. Withdrawal symptoms include mood swings, suicidal thoughts or attempts, fatigue, restlessness, loss of appetite, and sleeplessness. The potential for psychological addiction to steroids is high.

How can I keep up with the other athletes who use steroids?

ANSWER The majority of teen athletes aren't using steroids. Among teenage males (the group most likely to use steroids) only 1.8 percent of eighth graders, 2.3 percent of tenth graders, and 3.2 percent of twelfth graders reported steroid use in 2006. To really be a great athlete, focus on a proper diet, rest, good overall mental and physical health, and regular practice.

Craig's Story Continued

Craig's appearance was so important to him that he was willing to risk the dangers of steroid use. "The scale was my enemy. Every pound meant so much to me," he says. Craig constantly compared himself with others. He drove his friends and family crazy asking, "Is that guy bigger than me? What about that guy?" He was never completely satisfied. "Some days, I'd be arrogant, wearing shorts to show off my quads. Other days, I'd be a disaster. On a non-lifting day, I'd have to wear big, baggy clothes."

The drugs took their toll. Craig's hair fell out. Acne popped up all over his back. His face swelled. Then something even more serious happened: he started having chest pains. Craig was also having problems in his personal life. "I don't even remember how much of a jerk I was," he says. He alienated his friends and family. He was on the verge of losing all of his loved ones—and his own life. When he started, he had no idea that steroids would lead him down this path. He wanted to look good and be an exceptional athlete. Instead, Craig wound up needing the help of a psychiatrist to quit using the drug before he lost everything.

Craig's story is adapted from "Behind the Bulk: Craig's Story," by Cate Baily, in *Scholastic Choices*, April 2003.

Cocaine: Blayze's Story

One Saturday morning, Blayze, 15, dragged himself out of bed around 9:00 A.M. Before getting in the shower, he looked in the bathroom mirror and was horrified. "I looked terrible, totally unhealthy," Blayze says. "I had big dark circles under my eyes, and I was so skinny that I could see my rib cage."

Blayze hadn't always had a drug problem. In fact, up until the middle of his sophomore year, he played on three junior varsity school sports teams: soccer, basketball, and baseball. Then in April 2002, his friend Rich got some cocaine from his older brother and asked Blayze if he wanted to try it.

"I didn't know much about cocaine, and I figured it wasn't such a big deal," says Blayze, now 18. The two friends went behind their school that afternoon and snorted some of the white powder off a CD case. They got high and immediately planned to buy some more from the drug dealer to try it "just one more time," Blazye says.

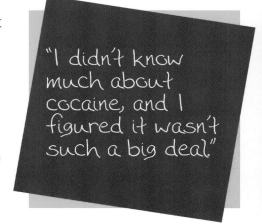

"I didn't know much about cocaine, and I figured it wasn't such a big deal"

However, cocaine use is not easy to control. Within two weeks of his first experience with the drug, Blayze was doing it almost every day. He was snorting it before, during, and after school. His weekends were spent doing the drug. As a result, he lost his appetite—sometimes he ate nothing but two candy bars a day—and he couldn't sleep.

He stopped playing sports and began cutting classes. His grades plummeted to Ds. On top of all that, he was forking over a couple of hundred dollars a week to his drug dealer—money that his parents and grandparents gave him after Blayze lied about school trips and expenses. He had become addicted to cocaine.

He had become **ADDICTED.**

THE **TRUTH** ABOUT
cocaine:
FAQs

QUESTION   How is crack different from cocaine?

ANSWER   Cocaine is a stimulant that is generally sold on the street in the form of a fine, white powder. Crack is the crystallized form of cocaine, and it's usually smoked in a pipe.

QUESTION   Why is cocaine dangerous?

ANSWER   Cocaine is a stimulant that speeds up your heart and causes your blood vessels to narrow. Cocaine use can cause irregular heart rhythms, heart attacks, chest pain, breathing problems, dangerous overheating called hyperthermia, strokes, seizures, headaches, abdominal pain, and nausea. It is also extremely addictive.

What are the effects of long-term cocaine abuse?

ANSWER Beyond addiction, frequent use of cocaine can have many bad effects including paranoia, aggressive behavior, and depression. Snorting the drug could burn permanent holes in the inside of the nose.

Frequent use of cocaine can cause **paranoia, aggressive behavior, and depression.**

Blayze's Story Continued

Blayze's story is a testament to how cocaine can take over a user's life. In October 2004, one of his friends got Blayze to try crack cocaine. "It was the biggest mistake I've ever made because I got immediately addicted," he says. Over the next three months, he smoked it whenever he could. Only after he was caught doing drugs at the end of 2004 did he finally get professional help to deal with his addiction.

In January 2005, Blayze entered a drug treatment facility. He hasn't done cocaine since and vows never to go anywhere near the drug again. "It did so much damage to my health, my school record, and to my family," he says.

These days, his life is much better. His weight is back up to a healthy 160 pounds. He recently graduated from high school and is currently majoring in telecommunications at a college in New Jersey. His days of doing cocaine appear to be behind him, and he doesn't want anyone else to do the drug. "Stay away," Blayze says. "Cocaine is dangerous, and it's so addictive it can make you lose control of your life."

Blayze's story is adapted from "Down and Out," by Leah Paulos, *Scholastic Choices*, February/March 2006.

Ecstasy: Daniel's Story

Daniel, 17, wanted prom night to be special. So he reached into his tuxedo pocket and took out pills stamped with images of Tweety Bird and the Buddha. Ecstasy looked harmless enough. But after Daniel took it, he found out how dangerous it can be.

"My heart was racing so fast. I thought I was having a heart attack," he says. A friend helped him into the prom because his legs wouldn't stop trembling. Then Daniel hit a peak. The prom was located on a Hollywood movie set, and there, Daniel started to tingle from head to toe. "I felt like a movie star," he said.

"My heart was racing so fast. I thought I was having a heart attack."

Later, at a friend's house, Daniel crashed into gloom and confusion. He swallowed two more pills. Taking additional doses within a relatively short time multiplies the toxic risks of any drug. With ecstasy, doubling the dose carries an especially high risk.

The level of ecstasy builds, and the user's body can't keep up with the amount of the drug in the bloodstream. That's what happened to Daniel. "I lay down and couldn't lift my head," he says. "My legs were rocking back and forth."

The following weekend, Daniel tried ecstasy again at an outdoor rave where some 200 kids danced on a dirt clearing. Before long, Daniel was selling ecstasy. "I'd walk into raves and yell 'E!' and people would crowd around. I felt a sense of power." With the profits, he bought more ecstasy, which he took often, always with other kids. "I did drugs so I didn't have to feel alone," he says.

THE **TRUTH** ABOUT
ecstasy:
FAQs

QUESTION How many teens use ecstasy?

ANSWER According to a 2001 NIDA-funded study, 5.2 percent of eighth graders had tried ecstasy; 8 percent of tenth graders had tried the drug; and 11.7 percent of twelfth graders had tried it.

QUESTION Why is ecstasy dangerous?

ANSWER Ecstasy users risk dehydration, dangerously high body temperature, kidney failure, and heart failure—all of which can be fatal. Unpleasant side effects include nausea, anxiety, teeth-clenching, blurred vision, depression, and paranoia. Because ecstasy users often lose their inhibitions, they can be more likely to take part in other risky behaviors.

QUESTION What is in ecstasy?

ANSWER When you buy ecstasy, you never really know what else may be in it. Pills sold as ecstasy contain MDMA, a hallucinogen. They often contain other substances as well. Recently, police labs have turned up heroin, cocaine, and even animal tranquilizers in so-called ecstasy pills.

QUESTION What are the side effects of using ecstasy?

ANSWER Ecstasy can damage a user's brain, causing memory and sleep problems and possibly depression. Ecstasy can destroy the fibers of neurons that carry serotonin, a chemical messenger that plays a big role in mood, pain, sleep, memory, and thinking.

QUESTION What about other "club drugs"?

ANSWER Some club drugs produce a sense of detachment from the user's surroundings or self—or even real unconsciousness. Because of these effects, these drugs are often used in date rapes. All club drugs can cause serious health consequences or, in some cases, death. Combining them with alcohol is especially dangerous. Common club drugs include:
- GHB (gamma-hydroxybutyrate) has euphoric, sedative, and anabolic (body-building) effects
- Ketamine, a drug commonly used as an animal tranquilizer
- LSD, or lysergic acid diethylamide, a hallucinogen

Daniel's Story Continued

Soon Daniel was taking up to five ecstasy pills a day. Desperate to feed his habit, he started selling cocaine and methamphetamine as well as ecstasy. "I was skinny. My skin was the color of paper. My teeth were rotting out," he said. "I would steal anything I could get my hands on. I stole valuables from my dad. I didn't see anything wrong with the way I was acting."

On New Year's Eve, Daniel's girlfriend called him a drug addict and a lowlife. He jumped out of her car. "Staring at the city hotels and gas stations, I thought 'I'm going to be living alone in the streets' and that scared the daylights out of me," Daniel recalled.

The next morning, he went to his father and said, "Dad, I need help."

Daniel entered a drug treatment center and has been clean for six months. He's gained weight, and he cares about himself again. But he worries about ecstasy's effects. "I feel like I've suffered brain damage," he said. "Sometimes I get stuck in conversations because I can't find a word."

Daniel's story is adapted from "Close-Up: Ecstasy,"
by Laura D'Angelo, in *Scholastic Choices*, February 2003.

Heroin: Judy's Story

You read about Judy's battle with heroin in Chapter 1. Here's more information about this deadly drug.

THE **TRUTH** ABOUT
heroin:
FAQs

QUESTION Is heroin dangerous when it's not injected?

ANSWER Yes. In any form, heroin can be deadly—and powerfully addictive.

QUESTION What are the non-fatal effects of using heroin?

ANSWER The risks are numerous, from nausea and vomiting to skin infections and loss of appetite. Heroin ravages the body, causing serious constipation, scarred veins, and breathing problems. The most serious risks include infection to the lining of the heart, irregular blood pressure, and a slowed heartbeat.

QUESTION Is there still a risk of getting AIDS or other diseases from heroin use?

ANSWER Often, heroin addicts will share needles, which can spread dangerous diseases like hepatitis B or C as well as HIV, the virus that causes AIDS.

QUESTION How many teens use heroin?

ANSWER In a recent study, only 1.5 percent of teens report using heroin. Use among teens has gone down by anywhere from one-half to two-thirds in the last ten years, but the rates have remained about the same since 2004.

Methamphetamine: Ricky's Story

You read about Ricky's methamphetamine addiction in Chapter 2. Here's more information about meth.

THE **TRUTH** ABOUT
Methamphetamine:
FAQs

QUESTION	Is meth more or less addictive than other drugs?
ANSWER	Like other drugs, crystal meth causes the brain to release extra amounts of dopamine. But meth releases more dopamine than other drugs—three or four times more than cocaine. That means you can get addicted faster. "It's so potent that I believe you can become addicted the first time you use it," says Dr. Nora Volkow of NIDA.

QUESTION Is meth use becoming more common among teens?

ANSWER In a recent study, only 8 percent of teenagers report having used meth. Teen meth use was actually down about a quarter over a ten-year period, but it hasn't changed much since 2003.

QUESTION Is meth as dangerous as other drugs?

ANSWER "It's the most harmful drug I've ever seen," says Jamie Van Leeuwen, director of public affairs for Urban Peak, a teen treatment center in Denver. Too much crystal meth damages your brain cells. Meth users can have severe memory loss along with trouble concentrating. Some meth users have heart attacks or strokes. "Imagine being 16 and having a stroke," says Volkow. "Imagine not being able to walk or talk again—for the rest of your life. That's what meth can do to you." Prolonged use may also result in violent or aggressive behavior, psychosis, and brain damage.

clean and sober

clean
and sober

"I HOPE I CAN FORGIVE MYSELF."

Quitting Drugs: Sam's Story

Sam is a 16-year-old girl from Michigan who once excelled in art and dancing. She doesn't remember ever fighting with her parents over anything more serious than her curfew time.

Sam started smoking marijuana at 13, and quickly moved on to prescription drugs. She stole Valium from her mom's medicine chest. She even raided her friend's bathrooms for everything from Ritalin to Vicodin to cough syrup. At 15, she discovered crystal meth. "That's all I wanted to do, 24/7," Sam says. "I didn't want to go to school. I didn't want to see my friends. I didn't want to dance. I just wanted to stay high all the time."

First Sam's grades dropped. Then she stopped going to school altogether. She ran away and lived on the streets for a week until police finally picked her up for stealing money from a Dairy Queen. A court ordered her to spend thirty days at a rehabilitation facility, but her parents signed her up for ninety. And before Sam knew it, she was one of thirty teenage drug addicts in a Florida clinic's adolescent wing.

Substance abuse is a hard habit to kick, no matter what drug you're using. More than 5 million teenagers use drugs each year—not including alcohol and tobacco. And about 30 percent of young people age 16 or over smoke regularly. It's clear that these teens need help. According to the National Center on Addiction and Substance Abuse, almost 8 percent of American teenagers need drug abuse treatment.

Most experts agree that it's hard, if not impossible, to quit a drug habit without professional counseling. Yet few teens willingly go to drug treatment. Their parents often notice the problem before they do and force them to get help. Other kids end up in rehab after they've run into trouble with the law. Experts say most kids in drug rehab have been arrested and referred to treatment by a court, a social services agency, or a probation officer.

30%

About 30 percent of young people age 16 or over smoke regularly.

For many teens, the best way to quit drugs is through counseling (individual and group) and other forms of **behavioral therapy**. In therapy, teens examine the reasons they started taking drugs. They build skills to resist drug use. Behavioral therapies help with relationships in the home and community.

For many kids, recovery also involves joining a 12-step program. This is a treatment technique that was made famous by Alcoholics Anonymous and has been adopted by groups ranging from Narcotics Anonymous and Alateen to Gamblers Anonymous and groups that deal with Internet addictions.These groups usually follow a similar route: Members meet regularly to discuss their experiences and give each other support. They treat addiction as an illness rather than a bad habit or a lack of willpower. The "steps" are phases addicts must complete. First, addicts admit they have a problem. Another step is "making amends"— saying they're sorry to the people they have hurt.

Members meet regularly to discuss their experiences and GIVE EACH OTHER SUPPORT.

Going Through the Motions

At first, Sam actually liked the idea of going to rehab. "I thought it would be like a vacation. Like a spa," she says. "I knew I was doing too many drugs. I thought I'd hang out here for a while. Give my body a little break. And then go off and do more drugs."

But the first day was a slap in the face. She was put through a strip search to make sure she didn't have drugs hidden on her body. All her possessions were taken away—including her jewelry, makeup, and clothes. The bedrooms were dormitory-style, with bunks and six people to a room. Everyone got up at 6 A.M., ate breakfast, and exercised. They spent the day going to school, getting drug treatment,

and doing chores. "I was on my knees cleaning toilets," Sam says. "That's the first time I've ever done anything like that."

Sam admits that at first she was not taking rehab seriously. She was "going through the motions," she says. It was easy to fool the other kids and counselors. "I've always been good at tricking people," she admits. Eventually, she sneaked away from the facility and hitchhiked to the beach. At her first opportunity, she got high again—and stayed high on meth for a week.

Eventually, Sam took a close look at what her life had become—and called the rehab center to come get her.

Sam began to work harder at rehab. Cleaning toilets and not being allowed to use her makeup still made her mad. But she swallowed her anger and tried to understand the point of these rules. "Part of it was learning discipline," she says. "I think another part was just keeping us busy so we didn't have time to think about drugs."

Sam began to enjoy the group counseling sessions. And for the first time, she came clean to her peers. She talked about the pressures she felt to be perfect in school and at home. And when the group felt like Sam was holding something back, they weren't shy about calling her on it. "It's hard to get used to people yelling at you," she laughs. Sam even dabbled with her artwork again.

"Part of rehab was learning discipline."

Still, Sam has a long way to go. In a few weeks, she'll move on to another program. She'll live outside the center but report to it each day for schoolwork and counseling. She'll also have to find a job. Her mom is flying down to Florida to stay with her. And Sam is more than a little nervous about seeing her again.

"I think she'll be proud of me, of all I've accomplished," Sam says. "I hope she'll forgive me. I hope I can forgive myself."

I hope she'll forgive me. I hope I can forgive myself.

QUITTING
is possible

QUITTING DRUGS ISN'T EASY.

In fact, it may be the hardest thing an addict ever does. Here's some advice experts have for someone who is trying to quit.

- Ask for help—from counselors, therapists, and your friends and family.

- Start going to a 12-step program.

- Tell your friends that you have stopped using drugs. Forget about the friends you did drugs with. Your true friends will respect your decision.

- Ask friends and family to be available when you need them. You may need to call someone in the middle of the night. When things get tough, don't try to handle them on your own. Accept the help your family and friends offer.

- Only go to places where you know drugs and alcohol won't be available. Skip the party Saturday night. Go to the movies or bowling instead.

- At some point, you'll find yourself in a place with drugs or alcohol. So have a plan. Rehearse what you'll say when someone offers you drugs or alcohol. Have a signal with a friend to communicate that you need to get out of there—now!

- If you slip, talk a counselor, therapist, or your sponsor in a 12-step program. You don't need to be ashamed. But you do need to try again. Recovery is hard work. But you are worth the effort!

Quitting Cigarettes: Sarah's Story

Think quitting smoking is easy? Just ask Sarah. She had smoked a pack a day since she was 14. She tells how she got through her initial smoke-free days.

This year, my college started a program with the American Lung Association to help teens quit. On day one, I told everybody I quit—but I didn't really. I only smoked two cigarettes, though. For me that's great. I think I was scared of quitting at first. Smoking was part of who I was.

I vowed to start over the next day and promised not to have even one cigarette. But by the time I woke up, I felt a real physical need to smoke. I was tense and crabby. I wanted a cigarette really, really bad. A week later, I could make it through a few days without a cigarette. But I was really irritable. I yelled at

my friends for stupid things. I even fell to pieces and started crying when I shrank a sweater in the dryer.

I vowed to start over the next day.

For days, I had a splitting headache. It was hard to concentrate in class. I kept seeing other students taking cigarette breaks. I fantasized about sneaking out and bumming a drag off their smokes. But I held back. I should have felt good about myself. But my whole body felt lousy. I felt like I had a dozen cravings an hour.

After two weeks, it was getting a little easier. But then I was in a car with friends driving to a movie. They were smoking. The smell made me a little sick. But I still took a drag from their cigarettes. After, I felt really guilty. I had been so good for so many days. Now it was like starting over.

But this time, after about three weeks I was much better at resisting temptation. I began adding up all the money I saved on cigarettes each week. I'd spend it on a special gift for myself—like clothes or music. I even took my boyfriend out to dinner! And he told me my hair didn't smell like smoke anymore.

Happy Endings!

There is hope for young addicts. Drug addiction is treatable. Over time, people can learn special skills and techniques to control their behavior. Many of the young people you read about in this book still struggle with their addiction. But they believe they have turned a corner. And as you can see from the end of their stories, they can imagine a drug-free life ahead of them.

Judy's Story

After hitting rock bottom because of her heroin abuse, Judy checked into a drug treatment facility. And while she has been drug-free for more than two months, her real struggles are just beginning. Even talking about heroin during her counseling sessions makes her want to start using again.

Judy knows that she'll always be an addict. But she's improving her relationships with people in her family and planning on going back to school to study accounting or interior design. "I want a life. I want a family. I want children," she says. "I want my parents to be proud of me. And the only way to do all that is to get off this stuff."

Ricky's Story

When we talked to Ricky he had been meth-free for a month. "It hasn't been easy," he says. "I have cravings every day. Some nights, I even dream about getting high." But Ricky says he's doing better. He might even be home for his prom and graduation. Until then, his mom and sister visit him in rehab on Sundays. "They tell me they love me and I just smile. I can barely look them in the eyes," he says. "You never know how much you can hurt somebody until you use crystal meth. I've got a long road ahead of me and a lot of fences to mend."

Lacy's Story

Lacy's parents forced her into counseling for her drinking after she was rushed to the ER with alcohol poisoning. Lacy has learned to look at her near-tragedy as a sign. She hasn't touched alcohol in two years. She's gotten her grades back up, but she feels uncomfortable at school. People still whisper about the time she almost died. But she says she's slowly regaining her self-esteem. And although her ex-boyfriend Peter has tried to be her friend, Lacy knows she can't go back to her old drinking crowd.

"I can't really blame them because I made these choices myself," she says. "But I was trying to change who I was to fit in with [Peter] and the cool group. I'm realizing how stupid that was. It almost cost me my life."

addiction—a chronic, relapsing disease in which people compulsively seek and use drugs and long-lasting chemical changes are made in the brain

amphetamines—stimulant drugs whose effects are similar to cocaine

behavioral therapy—therapy that focuses on solving patients' problems by making changes in their behavior

central nervous system—a system in the body that includes the brain and spinal cord and controls the actions of the body

cerebral cortex—the part of the brain responsible for cognitive (thinking) functions such as reasoning, mood, and strategy

depressants—drugs that acts on the central nervous system and slow brain activity

dopamine—a brain chemical that is released to create or stimulate feelings of pleasure

drugs—chemical compounds or substances that can alter the structure and function of the body

hallucinogens—a group of drugs that alter perceptions, thoughts, and feelings

hepatitis—inflammation of the liver

limbic system—the "reward" center of your brain; a set of brain structures that control good feelings and tell us when we like something

narcotics—addictive drugs that reduce pain and cause drowsiness and changes in mood

neurons—types of brain cells that process and transmit information throughout the brain

neurotransmitters—chemicals produced by neurons to carry messages to other neurons

steroids—manufactured testosterone-like drugs that are usually taken to build muscle and enhance athletic performance

stimulants—a class of drugs that act on the central nervous system and increase activity in the body and brain

tolerance—a condition in which higher doses of a drug are required to produce the same effect experienced when the user first tried the drug

withdrawal—symptoms that occur after use of an addictive drug is stopped

Books

Brigham, Janet. *Dying to Quit: Why We Smoke and How We Stop.* Washington, D.C.: Joseph Henry Press, 1998.

Kuhn, Cynthia, Scott Swartzwelder, and Wilkie Wilson. *Pumped: Straight Facts for Athletes About Drugs, Supplements, and Training.* New York: W. W. Norton & Company, 2000.

Vogler, Roger E. *Teenagers and Alcohol: When Saying No Isn't Enough.* Philadelphia: The Charles Press, 1992.

Videos

Moyers on Addiction: Close to Home
> This five-part PBS series from journalist Bill Moyers takes a look at addiction and recovery in America. Segments include "Real-Life Stories," "Science: The Hijacked Brain," "Treatment: Changing Lives," and "Prevention: The Next Generation." See: *www.wnet.org/closetohome/home.html*

Online Sites & Organizations

Action on Smoking and Health
www.ash.org
An antismoking and non-smokers' rights organization. Offers resources for information about smoking and health.

Al-Anon/Alateen
www.al-anon.alateen.org
An organization that offers hope and help to families and friends of alcoholics. Alateen caters specifically to teenagers.

Alcohol and Other Drug Information for Teens
www.child.net/drugalc.htm
This informational page by the National Children's Coalition offers facts about drugs and alcohol, teen recovery groups, and a drug and alcohol resource center.

Alcoholics Anonymous
www.aa.org
A group that helps alcoholics recover. The Web site lists symptoms of specific drugs and offers literature on sobriety and drinking.

Marijuana Anonymous
www.marijuana-anonymous.org
The official home page of MA helps young people determine whether they are addicted to marijuana. It provides information on the group's 12-step approach to recovery.

Narcotics Anonymous
www.na.org
NA is an international association of recovering drug addicts.

NIDA for Teens
teens.drugabuse.gov
NIDA—the National Institute on Drug Abuse—offers this science-based site for teens, with information, resources, facts and stats, and real-life stories.

Students Against Destructive Decisions (SADD)
www.sadd.org
SADD is a teen leadership organization dedicated to preventing underage drinking, impaired driving, and other drug use.

12-step programs, 92, 99

A

abuse, 12, 56
addiction
  alcohol, 46
  brain and, 29, 34, 37
  cocaine, 75, 76, 77, 78
  cravings and, 28, 34
  definition of, 13
  as disease, 13, 29
  dopamine and, 34, 42
  dosage and, 34, 37
  drug abuse and, 36
  escape and, 12
  genetics and, 37
  heroin, 8, 11, 84
  home life and, 12
  influences and, 18
  limbic system and, 34, 37
  marijuana, 53
  methamphetamine, 23–24, 86
  nicotine, 42, 43
  physical, 36, 53
  prescription drugs, 13, 62, 65
  psychological, 36, 37, 53, 70
  steroids, 70
  teen years and, 37
  tobacco, 40, 42, 43
  tolerance and, 34
  Xanax, 62
aerosols, 17
aggression, 70, 77, 87
AIDS, 85
Alateen, 92
alcohol, 13, 15, 18, 19, 28, 45, 46–47, 65, 82, 91, 103
alcohol poisoning, 47, 49
Alcoholics Anonymous, 92
allergic reactions, 69
"Amanda," 49–50, 55
American Lung Association, 100
amphetamines, 14
amyl nitrite, 17
anabolic steroids, 17, 68
animal tranquilizers, 82
antibiotics, 13
anxiety, 20, 81
appetite, 14, 25, 70, 75, 84
arrests, 27, 63, 91
asphyxiation, 58
asthma, 69
Ativan, 15

B

behavioral therapies, 92
benzene, 59, 60
bidis (flavored cigarettes), 43
binging, 25, 46
blackouts, 48, 59, 60
"Blayze," 73, 75, 78
blood pressure, 54, 84
body temperature, 81
bone marrow, 59, 60
boredom, 12, 21
boys, 19, 69
brain
  addiction and, 29
  dopamine, 34, 42, 52, 86
  hippocampus, 53
  hypothalamus, 69
  limbic system, 32–33, 34, 37, 70
  memory loss, 16, 45, 53, 54, 82, 87
  neurons, 30–31, 59, 82
  serotonin, 82
  stimulants and, 14
  toluene and, 59
breathing, 9, 47, 58, 65, 76, 84
butyl nitrite, 17

C

cancer, 43, 47, 70

Cannabinoids
  hashish, 16
  marijuana, 7, 9, 49–50,
    52–54, 89
car accidents, 47
Centers for Disease Control
    and Prevention (CDC),
    41
central nervous system, 14,
    60, 65
cerebral cortex, 32
chewing tobacco, 14, 43
chronic lung disease, 69
cigarettes, 14, 18, 39–41,
    42–43, 44, 100–101
cigars, 14, 43
"club drugs," 21, 82
cocaine, 14, 73, 75, 76–77, 82,
    83, 86
codeine, 16
cold medicines, 65
Columbia University, 64
cooking sprays, 17
correction fluids, 17, 60
Corrigall, Bill, 40
cough medicines, 65
crack cocaine, 14, 76, 78
"Craig," 67–68, 72
cravings, 9, 10–11, 13, 28, 34,
    101, 103
crime, 11, 36
crystal meth. See
    methamphetamine.
cysts, 70

D
"Daniel," 79–80, 83
death, 41, 43, 47, 58, 81, 82
dehydration, 81
deodorant sprays, 17
depressants, 15, 62
depression, 20, 21, 70, 77, 81,
    82

dextromethorphan (DXM), 65
dietary supplements, 68
dopamine, 33, 34, 42, 52, 86
dosage, 15, 34, 37, 65, 79
driving, 47, 54
drug abuse, 13, 36

E
ecstasy, 7, 15, 19, 21, 79–80,
    82, 83
emphysema, 43
escape, 12, 21
ether, 17
experimentation, 12

G
gases, 17
gasoline, 17, 59, 60
genetics, 29, 37
GHB (gamma-
    hydroxybutyrate), 82
girls, 19, 69
glues, 17, 60

H
hair sprays, 17
hallucinations, 54, 65
hallucinogens, 15
hashish, 16
hearing loss, 60
heart
  alcohol and, 47
  attacks, 65, 70, 76, 87
  disease, 43
  failure, 81
  heroin and, 84
  infections, 9
  marijuana and, 54
  nicotine and, 42
  rate, 65, 84
  rhythm, 76
hepatitis, 70, 85
heroin, 8–9, 10–11, 16, 28, 82,

84–85
Hexane, 60
hippocampus, 53
HIV, 70, 85
hormones, 54, 68, 69
"huffing." See inhalants.
human growth hormone
    (HGH), 17
hyperthermia, 76
hypothalamus, 69

I

immune system, 54, 60, 70
independence, 21
influences, 18, 20
inhalants, 17, 56, 58–60, 61

J

jail, 27, 66
"Judy," 7–8, 9–11, 102

K

ketamine, 82
"Kevin," 39–40, 44
kidneys, 60, 81
Kopner, Jean, 21

L

"Lacy," 45, 48–49, 103
limbic system, 32–33, 34, 37, 70
liver, 9, 47, 60, 70
LSD (lysergic acid
    diethylamide), 82
lungs, 42, 54

M

marijuana, 7, 9, 49–50, 52–54,
    89
MDMA, 82
"Megan," 56, 61
memory loss, 16, 45, 53, 54,
    82, 87
menstrual irregularities, 54, 69

mental illnesses, 29
methamphetamine, 14,
    23–27, 83, 86–87, 89, 103
Moolchan, Eric, 44
morphine, 16
mouth cancer, 47
mushrooms, 15
music, 21

N

Nandrolone Decanoate, 17
Narcotics Anonymous, 92
National Center on Addiction
    and Substance Abuse,
    91
National Institute on Drug
    Abuse (NIDA), 8, 29, 40,
    44, 81, 86
National Institutes of Health
    (NIH), 18, 19
nerve damage, 59, 60
neurons, 30–31, 82
neurotransmitters, 31, 32–33,
    34
"Nicole," 62–63, 66
nicotine, 13, 28, 39–41, 42, 43
Nicotine and Tobacco
    Addiction Program, 40
nitrites, 17
nitrous oxide, 17, 59, 60

O

O'Brien, Kimberley, 19, 20
opioids, 16
overdoses, 9, 15, 65
Oxandrolone, 17
OxyContin, 16

P

paint thinners, 17
paranoia, 54, 77, 81
parents, 9, 18, 19, 49, 50, 55, 62,
    66, 83, 89, 91, 97, 102, 103

peer pressure, 19, 44
Percocet, 16
Percodan, 16
physical addiction, 36, 53
pipe smoking, 14
prescription drugs, 63, 64–65, 66, 89
psychological addiction, 36, 37, 53, 70
puberty, 54

R
rehab. See treatment centers.
rehabilitation, 27, 90
respiratory disease, 54
respiratory failure, 58
"Ricky," 23–27, 28, 103
Rohypnol, 15
"roid rage," 70

S
"Sam," 89–90, 94–97
"Sarah," 100–101
Sasek, Catherine, 8
seizures, 76
self-esteem, 21, 103
serotonin, 82
side effects
    cocaine, 77
    ecstasy, 81, 82
    heroin, 84
    opioids, 16
skin conditions, 69
solvents, 17
spray paints, 17, 60
Stanozolol, 17
statistics
    alcohol, 46, 47
    drug use, 91
    ecstacy, 81
    heroin, 85
    methamphetamine use, 87

prescription drug abuse, 64
    smoking, 40, 42, 43
steroids, 67–68, 69–71
stimulants, 14
stress, 20
strokes, 76, 87
Sudden Sniffing Death, 58
suicide, 70

T
Teen Tobacco Addiction Treatment Research Clinic, 44
testosterone, 68
THC, 52
throat cancer, 47
tobacco, 91
tolerance, 34
Toluene, 59, 60
tranquilizers, 15
treatment centers, 55, 87, 91, 94–96, 103
Trichloroethylene, 60

U
University of Michigan, 64
Urban Peak treatment center, 87

V
vaccines, 13
Valium, 15, 89
Van Leeuwen, Jamie, 87
vision loss, 60
Volkow, Nora D., 29, 86, 87

W
whipped cream, 60
withdrawals, 36, 70

X
Xanax, 15, 62–63, 66

About the Author

John DiConsiglio is a writer in the Washington, D.C., area. He is the author of several books for young people, including *Coming to America: Voices of Teenage Immigrants* (Scholastic, 2002) and *Out of Control: How to Handle Anger—Yours and Everyone Else's* (Scholastic, 2008). As a journalist, he has covered some of the top stories of the last two decades, from presidential elections to Supreme Court decisions to the tragedy at Columbine High School. His work has appeared in numerous magazines, including *People*, *Glamour*, and *Cosmopolitan*. He is a graduate of Cornell University.